Shopping Trip

by Becky Cheston
illustrated by Peggy Collins

Scott Foresman
is an imprint of

Glenview, Illinois • Boston, Massachusetts • Chandler, Arizona
Upper Saddle River, New Jersey

Illustrations
Peggy Collins

Photographs
Every effort has been made to secure permission and provide appropriate credit for photographic material. The publisher deeply regrets any omission and pledges to correct errors called to its attention in subsequent editions.

Photo locators denoted as follows: Top (T), Center (C), Bottom (B), Left (L), Right (R), Background (Bkgd)

16 © DK Images

ISBN 13: 978-0-328-51367-3
ISBN 10:   0-328-51367-9

4 5 6 7 8 9 10 V0FL 15 14 13 12

Casey's baby sister Rose had been home for just one week. But already, Casey's excitement about having a new sister was wearing off. Rose never seemed to want to sleep—especially at night. And when Rose didn't want to sleep, that meant no one else could sleep, either.

On Saturdays, the family used to sleep late. They would eat pancakes, relax, and do their favorite activities. *Rose has changed everything,* thought Casey.

Dad was slumped in a chair, looking like he'd been struck by lightning. His hair stuck out every which way. Mom wore a gray nightgown that used to be pink. She could barely keep her eyes open. She was tired from doing housework and laundry. And Casey was curled up on the rug, daydreaming about life before Rose.

"I need some juice," Mom sighed.

"I'll get it," said Dad.

"Don't bother," said Casey. "We're out."

"Iced tea?" Mom asked. Poor Mom. She sounded so hopeful.

Casey gave her the bad news. "Nope. How about water?"

Casey got up and headed for the kitchen. She opened the refrigerator door. Besides the jug of spring water, there were two cartons of yogurt, three eggs, and an old head of lettuce that looked wilted and spoiled. "We need to go shopping," Casey announced.

"That's for sure," said Mom. "I'll go get dressed."

"You always do the shopping. Casey and I will go," Dad offered.

"Oh, thank you!" said Mom. "I'll make a list."

A crisp autumn breeze reddened their cheeks as Casey and Dad walked the three blocks to the supermarket. Inside the store, thousands of products lined the shelves. Dad wheeled a cart toward the endless line at the deli counter.

"This is a big list," said Dad, staring at Mom's shopping list in his hand. "Let's come back to the deli last. Maybe the line will be shorter."

Casey, who often shopped with Mom, knew her way around the supermarket. First, they picked out a variety of cheeses in the dairy section. Then, Casey led the way up and down the aisles.

In the diaper aisle, Dad grabbed the first box of diapers he saw and tossed it in their cart.

"Dad, I don't think these are the right size. Look at the baby on the front," said Casey.

Dad looked. "Hmm. She does look sort of big."

"And she's walking!" said Casey. She traded the big diapers for a pack labeled "Newborn."

After waiting for service at the deli counter, they waited in another line at the cash register. Finally, they paid, and walked out carrying their grocery bags. Dad looked at the list. "One more stop," he said. He led Casey across the street to the pet store.

"What are we doing *here*?" Casey asked.

"We need to get one more thing on the list," said Dad.

While Dad talked to the store clerk, Casey zipped right over to the puppies. Her heart melted. *Oh, if only*—but, Casey knew that now was not a good time to plead for a puppy.

When Casey and Dad returned, Rose was sleeping soundly. Casey bent next to the cradle and kissed one rosy cheek. Babies were great when they were sleeping.

In the kitchen, Mom unpacked the groceries. "Thanks for getting all this stuff," said Mom. She took another look in the empty grocery bags. "But, where are the crackers?"

"Crackers?" Dad asked.

"Yes, the tiny, cheesy ones that are shaped like goldfish."

A silly grin spread across Dad's face. "Oh." He held up a clear plastic bag half-filled with water. In it swam a bright orange goldfish.

"What should we do with it?" Mom asked, after they all stopped laughing.

"I'll take care of it," said Casey. It wasn't a puppy, but it was still a pet. "And I have just the name."

"What is it?" asked Mom and Dad together.

Casey smiled. "Cracker."

All About Bar Codes

Have you ever wondered what that small, square pattern of black bars and spaces on grocery products means? It is called a UPC bar code. There's one on the back of this book, too! The letters UPC stand for "Universal Product Code."

This code uses bars and spaces of different thicknesses to communicate information. When a cashier passes the bar code in front of the scanner, a light sensor decodes important details. Then, the scanner sends this information to a computer that is connected to the cash register. The computer tells the cash register what to charge for the item.

You know that bar codes can be found on grocery products and books. Where else can you find bar codes?

A bar code has all the important information about a product, including the price.

780863 185779